Press Release Distribution, Media Monitoring, Communication and Graphics services – Look No Further

The All-in-One Shop for Media and Communication Services

Send your Press Releases for Less and Get a Free Language Edition.

>> Increase your competitiveness with our packages

>> Be the news in every language

>> We take your news to local and global news media

>> Media contact and press release services

Media Monitoring, Analysis, and Measurement Services

>> TV and Radio News Monitoring

>> Online News and Social Media Monitoring

>> Monitor Competition

>> Measure PR & Marketing Effectiveness

>> Automate Daily, Weekly & Monthly Reports

Graphics and Communication Collateral Services

>> Print: Newsletters, Postcards, Calendar Design, Layout

>> Social Media: Campaign Management, Design

>> Website Design, Graphics

>> Video: Shooting, Producing, Editing

>> Advert/Media Buying Services

>> Printing Quotes

Start Today @ www.globalprplus.com
or Call: 1-832 857 2572

Editor's Comment

Changing the industry's supply chain behavior will go along way in helping the industry adapt in this low price environment. Putting it succinctly, Shell's Harry Brekelmans called on today's industry leaders to re-forge the links of supply chains to hammer out inefficiency, overpricing and arbitrariness.

The fact sheets on the new rule to curb methane emissions from the oil and gas industry- not limited to oil well sites but also at Natural Gas Transmission Compressor Stations, Natural Gas Production Gathering & Boosting Stations and Natural Gas Well Sites. The requirements the industry needs to put in place to find leak and repair pumps and compressors among all other technologies such as the optical gas imaging technology etc. This makes this edition a must read for all industry players and supply chain.

Still on regulations, the timeline for the well control safety rule is also out - we also have an independent organization to throw more light on the requirements of the new rule and its reporting requirements.

Technology providers from OTC- what new technologies they are offering the industry that could disrupt production while at the same time reducing cost are featured in this edition.

2017 International Pipeline, Oil and Gas Safety Conference will take place on March 14-17, 2017 at Houston Astro Minute Maid Park- Call for Abstracts and Early Bird Registration Opens. For more details: Jackie Smith @ +1 832 486 0095 or email: registration@oilandgassafetyconference.com

Take advantage of the free download period from Amazon and Get Your copy Today- Watch Your Email for the announcement.

Editor-in-Chief
Gloria Towolawi

Europe Bureau
Esther Coker

Nigeria Bureau
David Arhavbarien

Contributing Editor
Gloria Instead

Reporter
Caleb Motinwo

Advert & Marketing
Jewel Spring
T: 832-486-0095
E: advertise@usaoilandgasmonitor.com

Distribution & sales
Richard Godfirst

Subscribers Service
E: subscribe@usaoilandgasmonitor.com

RGT Media Communications Corp.
Publishers of
USA Oil and Gas Monitor
Workplace Weekly News
GlobalPRPlus

USA Oil and Gas Monitor is published 12 times a year monthly by RGT Media Communications Corp. 10777 Westheimer #1100

Houston, Texas 77042
Subscription price is $144 per year.
Digital copy $9.99 per download.

Copyright 2016 by
RGT Media Communications Corp.

All rights reserved. No part of this publication may be reproduced without the express permission in writing by the publisher or the original author.

Contents

Summary of Requirements for Processes and Equipment at Natural Gas Well Sites	4
Summary of Requirements for Processes and Equipment at Oil Well Sites	5
Summary of Requirements for Processes and Equipment at Natural Gas Production Gathering & Boosting Stations	8
Summary of Requirements for Processes and Equipment at Natural Gas Transmission Compressor Stations	9
Lloyd's Register Survey of oil and gas visitors at OTC Houston, Texas reveals 'adoption of new technologies'	11
EPA Releases Regulatory Standards to Cut Methane Emissions from the Oil and Gas Sector	12
Low Oil Price Environment Reveals "Dirty Little Secrets" of the Industry	14
Balancing CAPEX and OPEX along the Entire Value Chain- Siemens Solutions	18
ABS put BAVO Requirements into Perspective as Well Control Safety Rule enters Implementation Stage	21
BSEE Timeline for Implementation of the Well Control Rule	22
Alberta Wildfires Reduce Natural Gas Demand and Prices in Canada	24
Seven New DNV GL Collaborative Projects in North America	25
Purity Creates Design Opportunities: BQ-STEEL® AND IQ-STEEL®	26
Bearing Up In Oil and Gas - Help Cut Downtime and Boost Reliability	28
Photos from OTC 16	30

USA Oil and Gas Monitor
For Daily News Report and Analysis • www.usaoilandgasmonitor.com

Summary of Requirements for Processes and Equipment at Natural Gas Well Sites

EPA has issued final updates to its New Source Performance Standards NSPS for the oil and gas industry to reduce emissions of greenhouse gases – most notably methane – along with smog-forming volatile organic compounds VOCs from new, modified and reconstructed sources in the oil and natural gas industry. **At natural gas well sites, the updates add new requirements for detecting and repairing leaks, and requirements to limit emissions from pneumatic pumps.**

Finding and Repairing Leaks- Fugitive Emissions

- Leaks, also known as "fugitive emissions," can occur at a number of points at a natural gas well site when connections are not properly fitted, hatches are not properly weighted and sealed, or when seals and gaskets start to deteriorate. Leaks can be a significant source of methane and VOC emissions in the oil and gas industry.

The updated NSPS requires that owners/operators of natural gas well sites develop and implement a leaks monitoring plan. Owners/operators must use a technology known as optical gas imaging to conduct a leaks survey. Optical gas imaging equipment uses a special camera to "see" emissions of methane and VOCs.

Owners/operators may use "Method 21" as an alternative to optical gas imaging. Method 21 is an EPA method for determining VOC emissions from process equipment. The method is based on using a portable VOC monitoring instrument, such as an organic vapor analyzer sometimes referred to as a "sniffer".

- For new and modified well sites, owners/operators must conduct the initial survey one year after the final rule is published in the Federal Register, or within 60 days of the startup of production, whichever is later. After the first survey, leaks monitoring surveys must be conducted twice a year.

- The survey covers a number of components, including valves, connectors, pressure-relief devices, open-ended lines, flanges, closed vent systems, compressors and thief hatches on controlled storage tanks, among others.

- Any leaks found during the surveys must be repaired within 30 days, unless the repair would require shutting down production, which could lead to significantly greater emissions releases. In that case, owners/operators are required to fix the leak at the next shutdown, or within two years.

Equipment that vents natural gas as part of normal operation is not considered to be leaking and is not covered by this requirement; however, leaks surveys can also help operators detect malfunctions in these venting devices, such as pneumatic controllers.

- The final rule exempts some well sites that contain only wellheads known as "Christmas trees" from the leak detection and repair requirements.
- After considering public comment on the proposed rule, and based on available data, EPA is not exempting low-production well sites those with an average combined oil and natural gas production of less than 15 barrels of oil equivalent per well per day, from the requirements to find and repair leaks.
- Available data indicate that methane and VOC emissions from these sites could be similar to emissions from well sites that are not low-production. As a result, low-production well sites must meet the requirements of the leaks monitoring program.
- The final rule also creates a pathway for EPA to approve the use of emerging alternative leaks monitoring technology, which is developing rapidly. The rule outlines the information owners/operators must submit to demonstrate that using the alternative technology is capable of achieving methane and VOC reductions equivalent to those that can be achieved by using optical gas imaging or Method 21 to find leaks, and then repair them.

Pneumatic Pumps

- Pneumatic pumps use gas pressure to drive fluids. These pumps are used at natural gas production sites where electricity is not readily available. At natural gas well sites, pneumatic diaphragm pumps are used to transfer fluids or to circulate glycol "heat trace medium," which is used to keep pipes and equipment from freezing, for example.
- The final rule requires owners/operators of diaphragm pumps at natural gas well sites to route methane and VOC emissions from the pumps to a control device or process that is available on site, such as a device to control emissions from other equipment. Limited-use pneumatic pumps – those at a well site that operate for less than a total of 90 days per year – are exempt from the requirements. Owners/operators must meet these requirements within 180 days after the final rule is published in the Federal Register.
- Limited-use pneumatic pumps – those at a well site that operate for less than a total of 90 days per year – are exempt from the requirements. In addition, the rule clarifies that lean glycol circulation pumps are not covered by the pneumatic pumps standards.
- EPA is not finalizing requirements that owners/operators reduce emissions from natural gas-driven piston pumps, which are used to inject small amounts of chemicals to limit production problems and protect equipment. After analyzing currently available data and considering public comments on the proposed rule, EPA determined that these pumps are low-emitting and should not be subject to the final rule requirements.

Summary of Requirements for Processes and Equipment at Oil Well Sites

At oil productions sites, the updates set emission limits for completions of hydraulically fractured oil wells and pneumatic pumps, in addition to requirements for detecting and repairing leaks at oil well sites.

Requirements for New, Modified and Reconstructed Sources Not Covered in the 2012 Rules

Completions of Hydraulically Fractured Oil Wells

- Many hydraulically fractured wells that are drilled primarily for oil production contain natural gas along with the oil. During a stage of well completion known as "flow back," following the fracture of these wells, gas flows to the surface along with water, fracturing fluids, condensate and crude oil.
- The final rule requires owners/operators of hydraulically fractured oil wells to capture the natural gas that currently escapes into the air. Capturing the gas will both reduce methane and VOC emissions and maximize natural gas recovery from well completions.
- The rule requires that significant emissions reduction be accomplished primarily through the use of a proven process known as a "reduced emissions completion" or "green completion." This process is estimated to reduce methane and VOC emissions by 95 percent.

- In a green completion, special equipment separates gas and liquid hydrocarbons from the flow back that comes from the well as it is being prepared for production. The gas and hydrocarbons can then be treated and used or sold, avoiding the waste of natural resources that cannot be renewed.

Owners/operators must have a separator on site during the entire well completion process for development wells.

- EPA is phasing in the green completion requirement for hydraulically fractured oil wells to give the industry time to ensure that a sufficient supply of green completion equipment and personnel is available.
- Owners/operators will have six months after the final rule is published in the Federal Register to begin using green completions; they must reduce methane and VOC emissions using combustion controls until the green completion requirement takes effect.

Like the 2012 requirements for hydraulically fractured natural gas wells, the 2016 updates do not require green completions for certain oil wells, such as new exploratory "wildcat" wells, delineation wells used to define the borders of a reservoir, or low-pressure wells. A separator is not required to be on site for these wells; however, emissions from the wells must be controlled.

The final rule does not require emissions reductions from wells with a gas-to-oil ratio of less than 300 standard cubic feet of gas per barrel, provided the owner/operator maintains records of the low gas-to-oil ratio certification and a claim signed by a certifying official.

The rule also does not require green completions from other hydraulically fractured oil wells if it is not technically feasible to get the gas to a pipeline. Owners/operators of these wells generally must reduce emissions using combustion during the well-completion process.

- Oil wells that are re-fractured and recompleted are not be considered to be "modified" if well owners and operators use green completions to reduce emissions, and they meet notification and reporting requirements for new wells. This also was a requirement for completions of hydraulically fractured natural gas wells in the 2012 rules.

In a number of states, this allows owners/operators to re-fracture wells without triggering state permitting requirements. This flexibility reduces burden to both industry and permitting agencies, without compromising the environmental benefits of the rule.

Finding and Repairing Leaks Fugitive Emissions

- Leaks, also known as "fugitive emissions," can occur at a number of points at an oil well site when connections are not properly fitted, hatches are not properly weighted and sealed, or when seals and gaskets start to deteriorate. Leaks can be a significant source of methane and VOC emissions in the oil and gas industry.
- The updated NSPS requires that owners/operators of oil well sites develop and implement a leaks monitoring plan. Owners/operators must use a technology known as optical gas imaging to conduct a leaks survey. Optical gas imaging equipment uses

a special camera to "see" emissions of methane and VOCs.

Owners/operators may use "Method 21" as an alternative to optical gas imaging. Method 21 is an EPA method for determining VOC emissions from process equipment. The method is based on using a portable VOC monitoring instrument, such as an organic vapor analyzer sometimes referred to as a "sniffer".

For new and modified oil well sites, owners/operators must conduct the initial survey one year after the final rule is published in the Federal Register, or within 60 days of the startup of production, whichever is later. After the first survey, leaks monitoring surveys must be conducted twice a year.

The survey covers a number of components, including valves, connectors, pressure-relief devices, open-ended lines, flanges, closed vent systems, compressors and thief hatches on controlled storage tanks, among others.

Any leaks found during the surveys must be repaired within 30 days, unless the repair would require shutting down production, which could lead to significantly greater emissions releases. In that case, owners/operators are required to fix the leak at the next shutdown, or within two years.

Equipment that vents natural gas as part of normal operation is not considered to be leaking and is not covered by this requirement; however, leaks surveys can also help operators detect malfunctions in these venting devices, such as pneumatic controllers.

After considering public comment on the proposed rule, and based on available data, EPA is not exempting low-production well sites those with an average combined oil and natural gas production of less than 15 barrels of oil equivalent per well per day, from the requirements to find and repair leaks. Available data indicate that methane and VOC emissions from these sites could be similar to emissions from well sites that are not low-production. As a result, low-production well sites must meet requirements of the leaks monitoring program.

- The final rule also creates a pathway for EPA to approve the use of emerging alternative leaks monitoring technology, which is developing rapidly. The rule outlines the information owners/operators must submit to demonstrate that using the alternative technology is capable of achieving methane and VOC reductions equivalent to those that can be achieved by using optical gas imaging or Method 21 to find leaks, and then repair them.

Pneumatic Pumps

- Pneumatic pumps use gas pressure to drive fluids. These pumps often are used at oil production sites where electricity is not readily available. At well sites, pneumatic diaphragm pumps are used to transfer fluids or to circulate glycol "heat trace medium," which is used to keep pipes and equipment from freezing, for example.
- The final rule requires owners/operators of diaphragm pumps at natural gas well sites to route methane and VOC emissions from the pumps to a control device or process that is available on site, such as a device to control emissions from other equipment. Owners/operators must meet these requirements within 180 days after the final rule is published in the Federal Register.
- Limited-use pneumatic pumps – those at a well site that operate for less than a total of 90 days per year – are exempt from the requirements.
- EPA is not finalizing requirements that owners/operators reduce emissions from natural gas-driven piston pumps, which are used to inject small amounts of chemicals to limit production problems and protect equipment. After analyzing currently available data and considering public comments on the proposed rule, EPA determined that these pumps are low-emitting and should not be subject to the final rule requirements.
- The final rule encourages owners/operators to use pumps that are not driven by natural gas where technically feasible. These pumps include solar-powered, electrically powered and air-driven pumps, which are exempt from requirements of the rule.

Compressors

- EPA did not establish requirements for compressors at oil well sites, because these compressors are typically small and low emitting. However, compressors at oil gas well sites are included in the equipment covered by the leaks survey and repair requirements.

Requirements for Equipment Covered by the 2012 Rules

- The final updates to the NSPS add greenhouse gas standards, in the form of limitations on methane, for the types of equipment and processes that were covered in the 2012 NSPS for VOCs. EPA's analyses have determined that best systems for reducing methane and VOC emissions are the same. As a result, the final requirements for pneumatic controllers remain the same as in the 2012 rule.
- In addition, the 2012 rules included requirements for storage tanks across the oil and gas sector. The 2016 final NSPS does not change those requirements.

USA Oil and Gas Monitor
For Daily News Report and Analysis • www.usaoilandgasmonitor.com

Summary of Requirements for Processes and Equipment at Natural Gas Production Gathering & Boosting Stations

Gathering and boosting compressor stations collect gas from multiple wells and move it toward a natural gas processing plant. **For these stations, the final updates add requirements for detecting and repairing leaks.**

Finding and Repairing Leaks

- Leaks, also known as "fugitive emissions," can occur at a number of points at a natural gas gathering and boosting station when connections are not properly fitted, hatches are not properly weighted and sealed, or when seals and gaskets start to deteriorate. Leaks can be a significant source of methane and VOC emissions in the rapidly growing oil and gas industry.

- The final NSPS requires that owners/operators of gathering and boosting stations develop and implement a leaks monitoring plan. Owners/operators must use a technology known as optical gas imaging to conduct a leaks survey. Optical gas imaging equipment uses a special camera to "see" emissions of methane and VOCs.

Owners/operators may use "Method 21" as an alternative to optical gas imaging. Method 21 is an EPA method for determining VOC emissions from process equipment. The method is based on using a portable VOC monitoring instrument, such as an organic vapor analyzer sometimes referred to as a "sniffer".

- The leaks survey covers a number of components, including valves, connectors, pressure-relief devices, open-ended lines, flanges, compressors and thief hatches on controlled storage tanks, among others.

- Owners/operators must conduct an initial leaks survey within one year after the final rule is published in the Federal Register or within 60 days of the startup of a new or modified gathering and boosting station, whichever is later. Monitoring must be repeated quarterly following the initial survey.

- Any leaks found during the surveys must be repaired within 30 days, unless the repair would require shutting down production. In that case, owners/operators are required to fix the leak at the next scheduled shutdown, or within two years. o Equipment that vents natural gas as part of normal operation is not considered to be leaking and is not be covered by this requirement; however, leaks surveys can also help operators detect malfunctions in these devices, such as pneumatic controllers.

- The final rule also creates a pathway for EPA to approve the use of emerging alternative leaks monitoring technology, which is developing rapidly. The rule outlines the information owners/operators must submit to demonstrate that using the alternative technology is capable of achieving equivalent methane and VOC reductions that can be achieved by using optical gas imaging or Method 21 to find leaks, and then repair them.

New & Modified Pneumatic Pumps

- EPA is not finalizing requirements for pneumatic pumps used at gathering and boosting stations. After considering information that became available during the comment period on the proposed rule, EPA has determined that the agency does not have reliable information about the prevalence of pneumatic pump use at these sites at this time.

-

Requirements for Equipment Covered by the 2012 Rules

- The final updates to the NSPS add greenhouse gas standards (in the form of methane emissions limits) for the equipment and processes that were covered in the 2012 NSPS for VOCs. EPA's analyses have determined that the best systems for reducing methane and VOC emissions are the same. As a result, the final requirements for new, modified and reconstructed centrifugal and reciprocating compressors and the requirements for pneumatic controllers, remain the same as in the 2012 rule.

- In addition, the 2012 rules included requirements for storage tanks across the oil and gas sector. The 2016 final NSPS does not change those requirements.

- The final rule encourages owners/operators to use pumps that are not driven by natural gas where technically feasible. These pumps include solar-powered, electrically-powered and air driven pumps, and are exempt from requirements of the rule.

Compressors

- EPA did not establish requirements for compressors at natural gas well sites, because these compressors are typically small and low emitting. However, compressors at natural gas well sites are included in the equipment covered by the leaks survey and repair requirements.

Requirements for Equipment Covered by the 2012 Rules

- The final updates to the NSPS add greenhouse gas standards, in the form of limitations on methane, for same the types of equipment and processes that were covered in the 2012 NSPS for VOCs. EPA's analyses have determined that best systems for reducing methane and VOC emissions are the same. As a result, the requirements for completions of hydraulically fractured natural gas wells and pneumatic controllers, remain the same as in the 2012 rule.

- In addition, the 2012 rules included requirements for storage tanks across the oil and gas sector. The 2016 final NSPS does not change those requirements.

Summary of Requirements for Processes and Equipment at Natural Gas Transmission Compressor Stations

The updates affect some equipment at natural gas transmission compressor stations, which move gas along a pipeline. In addition to compressors, compressors stations often include equipment to remove and store water vapor, condensate and other remaining impurities

The updates add requirements for detecting and repairing leaks, and requirements to limit emissions from compressors and pneumatic controllers used at compressor stations.

Requirements for New, Modified and Reconstructed Sources Not Covered in the 2012 Rules

Compressors

- Compression is necessary to move natural gas along a pipeline. The 2016 final rule sets requirements to control greenhouse gases through a limit on methane emissions and VOCs from two types of compressors used at natural gas compressor stations: centrifugal compressors and reciprocating compressors.

- Centrifugal compressors - Centrifugal compressors are equipped with either wet seal systems, or dry seal systems.

Compressors with wet seals use oil as a barrier to keep gas from escaping. The gas that becomes absorbed in the oil is continuously vented, along with the methane, VOCs and air toxics it contains. The final rule requires a 95 percent reduction of methane and VOC emissions from compressors with wet seal systems. This can be accomplished through flaring, or by routing captured gas back to a process.

Compressors using dry seal systems, which have low methane and VOC emissions, are not covered by the final rule. EPA encourages owners/operators to use compressors with dry seal systems where possible.

- Reciprocating compressors – The final rule requires the replacement of rod packing systems in reciprocating compressors. Over time, these packing systems can wear, leaking methane and

VOCs. The rule provides two options for replacing rod packing:

On or before every 26,000 hours of operation operating hours must be monitored and documented; or every 36 months monitoring and documentation of operating hours not required.

- As an alternative to changing rod packing, operators may opt to route emissions from the rod packing via a closed vent system under negative pressure to be reused or recycled by a process or piece of equipment.
- The final rule also includes requirements for recordkeeping and annual reporting.

Pneumatic Controllers

- Pneumatic controllers are automated instruments used for maintaining liquid levels, pressure and temperature. These controllers often are powered by high-pressure natural gas and may release gas including methane and VOCs with every valve movement, or continuously, in many cases, as part of their normal operations.

For continuous bleed, gas-driven controllers, the final rule sets a gas bleed limit of 6 standard cubic feet of gas per hour at an individual controller.
Low-bleed controllers used at compressor stations with a gas bleed rate of 6 standard cubic feet per hour or less are not subject to this rule.

- The rule includes exceptions for applications requiring high-bleed controllers for certain purposes, including operational requirements and safety. The rule also includes requirements for recordkeeping and annual reporting.

Finding and Repairing Leaks- Fugitive Emissions

- Leaks, also known as "fugitive emissions," can occur at a number of points at a compressor station when connections are not properly fitted or when seals and gaskets start to deteriorate. Leaks can be a significant source of methane and VOC emissions in the oil and gas industry.
- The updated NSPS requires that owners/operators of compressor stations develop and implement a leaks monitoring plan. Owners/operators must use a technology known as optical gas imaging to conduct a leaks survey. Optical gas imaging equipment uses a special camera to "see" emissions of methane and VOCs.

Owners/operators may use "Method 21" as an alternative to optical gas imaging. Method 21 is an EPA method for determining VOC emissions from process equipment. The method is based on using a portable VOC monitoring instrument, such as an organic vapor analyzer sometimes referred to as a "sniffer".

- For new and modified compressor stations, owners/operators must conduct the initial survey within one year after the final rule is published in the Federal Register or within 60 days of the startup of a new or modified compressor station, whichever is later. Monitoring must be repeated quarterly following the initial survey.
- The survey covers a number of components, including valves, connectors, pressure-relief devices, open-ended lines, flanges, compressors, and thief hatches on controlled storage tanks, among others.
- Any leaks found during the surveys must be repaired within 30 days, unless the repair would require shutting down. In that case, owners/operators are required to fix the leak at the next scheduled shutdown, or within two years. o Equipment that vents natural gas as part of normal operation is not considered to be leaking and is not be covered by this requirement; however, leaks surveys can also help operators detect malfunctions in these devices, such as pneumatic controllers.

• The final rule also creates a path for EPA to allow use of alternative leaks monitoring technology, which is developing rapidly. The rule outlines the information owners/operators must submit to show that using the alternative technology is capable of achieving equivalent methane and VOC reductions that can be achieved by using optical gas imaging or Method 21 to find leaks, and then repair them.

Pneumatic Pumps

- EPA is not finalizing requirements for pneumatic pumps used at compressor stations. After considering information in the record and comments on the proposed rule, EPA has determined information about the prevalence of pneumatic pump use at compressor stations is not reliable at this time.

Storage Tanks

- The 2012 rules included requirements for storage tanks across the oil and gas sector. The 2016 final NSPS does not change those requirements.

Lloyd's Register Survey of oil and gas visitors at OTC Houston in Texas reveals 'adoption of new technologies' as the critical business issue in the next 18 months

We have spent this week at OTC Houston 2016 challenging oil and gas companies to re-think their approach to technical innovation, performance and safety to secure the world's energy supply in a sustainable way, from reservoir and refinery to beyond.

Our survey of exhibitors at OTC Houston 2016 revealed more than 43 per cent of respondents consider Adoption of new technologies including additive manufacturing or 3D Printing and the use of unmanned robotics to be the primary issue.

Using new technologies from other industries 17per cent; Better collaboration within the industry 16per cent; Data rationalization and interpretation techniques 13per cent; and Education initiatives for graduates and new industry entrants 11per cent, were also seen to be important issues.

So what can industry do? The answer lies in a sharper focus on driving excellence by collaborating and increasing the interconnected global network of knowledge across the energy and marine industries.

"It is widely accepted that excellence through innovation is key to safe and profitable growth across industry – and that collaboration can accelerate the development of innovative new technologies to help support better and cheaper ways of extracting and supplying energy," says Teril Smith, Senior Vice President of Lloyd's Register Energy in Houston, Texas.

According to our annual 2015-16 Oil & Gas Technology Radar survey, which researches the latest opinion of oil and gas executives across the world, "operational efficiency" is now the top driver for innovation investment. "Improving access to potential reserves" and "increasing the life span of assets" also rated more highly as innovation drivers this year compared to the previous 12 months, suggesting that, as well as nudging down the bottom line, companies are looking to push up the top line by extracting maximum value from resources.

What's next?

We believe our role in developing partnerships between industry and academia is important to help nurture collaboration and innovation, shown recently by our Global Technology Centre based out of Singapore, which is driving research in to how data can be used to improve integrity; the use of Unmanned Aerial Systems for faster and cost-effective inspection, plus our leading joint industry projects such as the role additive manufacturing can have in the manufacture of quality engineered components used in the energy and marine industries.

The offshore sector is rapidly realigning in response to the low oil price environment and other challenging dynamics. The issues appear to be well-understood, aided by good-quality dialogue and increased collaborative efforts.

"In this environment, staying afloat requires a new type of inventiveness and open mindedness; an eager and proactive search for novel technologies, approaches and ways of working," highlights Smith.

EPA Releases Regulatory Standards to Cut Methane Emissions from the Oil and Gas Sector

As a further step in the Obama Administration's commitment to take action on climate change and protect public health, the U.S. Environmental Protection Agency EPA is announcing comprehensive steps to address methane emissions from both new and existing sources in the oil and gas sector. For new, modified and reconstructed sources, EPA is finalizing a set of standards that will reduce methane, volatile organic compounds VOCs and toxic air emissions in the oil and natural gas industry. EPA is also starting the process to control emissions from existing sources by issuing for public comment an Information Collection Request ICR that requires companies to provide the information that will be necessary for EPA to reduce methane emissions from existing oil and gas sources.

"We are underscoring the Administration's commitment to finding commonsense ways to cut methane—a potent greenhouse gas fueling climate change—and other harmful pollution from the oil and gas sector," said EPA Administrator Gina McCarthy. "Together these new actions will protect public health and reduce pollution linked to cancer and other serious health effects while allowing industry to continue to grow and provide a vital source of energy for Americans across the country."

This actions are part of the Administration's strategy under President Obama's Climate Action Plan to reduce methane emissions, and keeps the Administration on track to achieve its goal of cutting methane emissions from the oil and gas sector by 40 to 45 percent from 2012 levels by 2025.

Methane, the key constituent of natural gas, is a potent greenhouse gas GHG with a global warming potential more than 25 times greater than that of carbon dioxide. Methane is the second most prevalent GHG emitted in the United States from human activities, and nearly one-third of those emissions comes from oil production and the production, transmission and distribution of natural gas.

The final standards will significantly curb methane emissions from new, reconstructed and modified processes and equipment, along with reducing VOC emissions from sources not covered in the agency's 2012 rules. These sources include hydraulically fractured oil wells, some of which can contain a large amount of gas along with oil, and equipment used across the industry that was not regulated in the 2012 rules.

After reviewing the more than 900,000 comments received on its August 2015 proposal, EPA updated a number of aspects in the final rule that increase climate benefits, including removing an exemption for low production wells and requiring leak monitoring surveys twice as often at compressor stations, which have the potential for significant emissions. The final rule also provides companies a pathway to align the final standards with comparable state-specific requirements they may have.

The final standards for new and modified sources are expected to reduce 510,000 short tons of methane in 2025, the equivalent of reducing 11 million metric tons of carbon dioxide. Natural gas that is recovered as a result of the rule can be used on site or sold. EPA estimates the final rule will yield climate benefits of $690 million in 2025, which will outweigh estimated costs of $530 million in 2025. Reductions in VOCs and air toxics are also expected to yield benefits; however EPA was not able to quantify those benefits.

The standards also are expected to reduce 210,000 short tons of ozone-forming VOCs in 2025, along with 3,900 tons of air toxics, such as benzene, toluene, ethylbenzene and xylene. Ozone is linked to a variety of serious public health effects, including reduced lung function, asthma attacks, asthma development, emergency room visits and hospital admissions, and early death from respiratory and cardiovascular causes. Air toxics are known or suspected to cause cancer and other serious health effects.

These final actions also include two rules that clarify permitting requirements for the oil and natural gas industry: the Source Determination Rule and a final federal implementation plan for the Minor New Source Review Program in Indian Country.

Over the past year, new science and data have shown that methane emissions from existing oil and gas sources are substantially higher than was previously understood. To build on the agency's current knowledge, EPA is issuing an ICR that seeks a broad range of information, including the types of technologies that could be used to reduce emissions and their associated costs. The information the agency receives in response to the ICR will provide the foundation for developing regulations to reduce methane emissions from existing oil and gas sources.

EPA will collect the information through a general survey for all owners/operators of existing sources and a more detailed survey for specific facilities. EPA anticipates receiving data from the operator survey later this year and expects to conclude all aspects of the ICR in the first part of 2017. In addition, the agency is announcing plans to issue a voluntary Request for Information to seek information on innovative strategies that can accurately and cost-effectively locate, measure and mitigate methane emissions.

Earlier this year, EPA launched the Methane Challenge Program, which provides a new way for U.S. oil and gas companies to achieve— and be recognized for—ambitious commitments to reduce methane emissions. This flexible program has the potential to foster significant cost-effective emission reductions across the oil and gas sector and to provide transparency on the progress partner companies are making to reduce emissions.

Advertise With Us

USA Oil and Gas Domain Analysis- For Online Advert Placement
Google Page Rank 4: An authority site for oil, gas and energy news
Global Rank Worldwide: 14,838,812
Estimated Monthly Visit: 2.5 million
Search: 94.68%
Source: Checkpagerank.net

New! Our Digital Edition is distributed by Amazon Kindle Select- Guarantees 1 billion Audience Reach.

Print Advert

Distributes: 4000 copies
Digital Edition Viewed by: More than 20,000 persons
Download media kit: http://usaoilandgasmonitor.com/advertise
Call Advert Hotline: 832-486-0095

USA Oil and Gas Monitor
For Daily News Report and Analysis • www.usaoilandgasmonitor.com

Harry Brekelmans, Projects & Technology Director, Royal Dutch Shell plc

Low Oil Price Environment Reveals "Dirty Little Secrets" of the Industry
Shell's Harry Brekelmans Calls for Change in Industry's Supply Chain Behavior

Speaking at the Offshore Technology Conference Mr. Harry Brekelmans said that the fall in crude-oil price has had quite an impact on the cash flow of not only the operators of oil and gas fields but also the companies that provide supplies and services to the operators. The situation has also revealed some "dirty little secrets" of the industry such as: **inefficiencies, overpricing and arbitrary risk allocation in the design, planning and construction of oil and gas projects.**

Giving that backdrop, he called on today's industry leaders to re-forge the links of supply chains to hammer out inefficiency, overpricing and arbitrariness. These were picked up over the last decade, when the industry chased oil and gas production on the back of economic expansion. At that time, the industry had sights set on more barrels rather than higher returns. The industry was convinced that global demand growth would see it through.

But this has left the industry today with baggage that drags down the industry's performance. The industry must now jettison that baggage in order to survive today's business environment and emerge reinvigorated from it. And this requires much deeper collaboration among industry players. He said, "We'll have to fundamentally change the way we interact with one another".

Capital and Labor Intensity

It's easy to blame the industry's current malaise on the sunken oil price, which since 2014 has been way below its 10-year average. But frankly, much of what afflicts the industry is of its own doing – and it predates 2014 by more than 10 years.

Over the many years that operators have been working together, both inside and outside respective companies –; Mr. Harry said, "our behavior have allowed cost, risk and inefficiency to spread unchecked across the industry's supply chain. There's been a vast expansion in project documentation and assurance processes, resulting in a proliferation of company-specific requirements. We have set up too many interfaces within and between companies and fragmented our work packages too much. The cumulative effect of all this largely explains why a barrel of oil today requires between three and four times more capital than a barrel produced in 2004".

In addition, there are factors beyond control at work too. For example, the hydrocarbon resources that are being developed today tend to be in more complex geological settings and in deeper water than they were a decade ago. And the economic boom in countries such as China, as well as massive projects in countries such as Australia, have also overheated markets for building materials and construction workers. This has resulted in higher prices and wages.

But those factors do not explain the increase in the amount of engineering man-hours per piece of equipment. The data show that, over the last 10 years, Shell engineers have become less efficient in designing onshore and downstream projects. And that worries me a lot, Harry said.

He continued, "But it is not just Shell engineers who have become less productive. It is the entire oil and gas industry. *Averaged around the world, it takes about 15 per cent more people to produce a barrel of oil today than it did 10 years ago.*

Now, you could say: "Well, that's what you get when governments impose more regulations on projects to protect the environment or to source local manpower and materials." **But then how do you explain the fact that other heavy industries have managed to avoid such performance-killing trends?**

If you compare the productivity of the automotive industry with that of the oil and gas industry, you will see that the trends go in opposite directions. Surely the US automotive industry has also been subject to as much government regulation as the US oil and gas industry"!

The uncomfortable truth is that the industry got itself into this current predicament. And the industry is capable of getting itself out of it. By deliberately, openly, creatively stripping out waste and creating new sources of value for oil and gas projects, the industry can secure its continued viability.

So how does the industry do that?

Mr. Harry said, "The industry can begin at the beginning – with the scoping of projects. This lies mostly in the hands of the operators, who specify what a project entails. For far too long, we have been satisfied with specifications that were too vague or that were left as a hostage to fortune".

The design and technical specification of a project should – first and foremost – be aimed at assuring a minimum acceptable performance. Scope changes to give a project greater value – say, by increasing its throughput – or to give it greater robustness against risks – say, by increasing its operational flexibility – must then only be accepted with full awareness of the cost trade-off. Above all, the project must be kept competitive vis-à-vis comparable projects. Shell refers to this as "competitive scoping".

For example he said that Shell recently built up a competitively scoped project for a mid-size development in the Gulf of Mexico. When all scope changes were accepted with eyes wide open as to their cost and value implications, capital-expenditure savings of 15 – 25 per cent were obtained – primarily from the scoping of

> *Averaged around the world, it takes about 15 per cent more people to produce a barrel of oil today than it did 10 years ago.*

the offshore platform as well as subsea pipelines and risers.

On industry standards he said…

Shell is also looking at ways to determine when something truly exceptional might be required to guarantee a project's success. In some cases, simply meeting industry norms may be enough. And the norms do not necessarily have to be set by the oil and gas industry.

The shipbuilding industry, for example, has come up with its own set of international standards. Could not they be adopted for engineering ship-like parts of a floating LNG facility – the hull and main deck, for example? He asked.

When a Shell project team answered "yes" to that question, it managed to reduce the number of requirements from 3,268 to 770 for the case of marine deaerators, which remove dissolved gases from boiler feed water. And that resulted in $50 million savings in shipyard scope. The project team would have faced not only higher costs but also potentially longer delivery times had it applied all of Shell's Design and Engineering Practices instead.

He adds, in many other areas the oil and gas industry has developed tried-and-tested practices and designs that are fit for purpose. But even there the supply chain can extract further value. That's why Shell recently joined nine other oil and gas producers to kick off a joint industry project with the aim of harmonizing company requirements. Initially, the project will focus on the specification of ball valves, subsea equipment and low-voltage switchgear.

And it is not only owner-operators who will benefit from such steps towards standardization. Suppliers also will reap benefits from easier packaging and delivery, simpler bidding processes and economies of scale in fabrication and testing.

No harm, no leaks, no waste- referring to safety requirements

Safety is top priority. But safety is about mindfully reducing risks, not mindlessly adding requirements into a management system. And I think the industry can cite instances where additional imposed requirements have done little to improve a project's safety but certainly introduced inefficiency. *"Safety is about mindfully reducing risks, not mindlessly adding requirements into a management system."* He exclaimed.

He opined that in some cases additional requirements have actually detracted from safety. There simply are too many requirements to keep track of. Consequently, it's easy for them to be duplicated – albeit imperfectly. At worst, this can lead to contradiction; at best, to confusion.

Shell operating companies in various countries have piled up a "mountain range" of paperwork into contracts with the best of intentions: to make lifting and hoisting safer. All in all, it consist of nearly 1,000 pages of documents. He said, "Shell's functional leadership believes that fewer than two dozen pages are sufficient to this end? The details of implementation should be left to those who are actually doing the lifting and hoisting".

He quickly adds, "We should never lose sight of the real goal behind our safety requirements – no harm, no leaks. But through initiatives such as Shell's Safety Leadership forums, we must dare to address areas where we have added cost and complexity without really reducing HSSE risk".

The crucial question the industry has to answer is how to meet safety's Goal Zero while cutting out waste, minimizing idle time and eliminating duplication of effort. The same applies to the assurance of the quality of a project's components. In fact, safety and quality performance go hand in hand.

Final Conclusion- Candid collaboration- change in industry's supply change behavior

New technology, efficient management and competitive scoping – in and of themselves – can certainly help to improve our industry's

> Safety is about mindfully reducing risks, not mindlessly adding requirements into a management system.

performance. Thanks to them, Shell is on course to deliver $4 billion of structural capital-investment savings over 2015 and 2016.

But they alone are not enough. The industry can – and must – deliver more. To sustained multibillion-dollar across-the-board improvements in capital efficiency. To have that kind of impact on the industry as a whole, the industry has to fundamentally change its behaviors in the supply chain.

The industry faces some harsh realities: capital investment is drying up; thousands of our colleagues are leaving the industry. High costs, low productivity, eroding competence, increasing safety micromanagement and decreasing quality control only add to that toll.

As a consequence, the industry's supply chain is being stretched to the breaking point. The situation can only be relieved through healthier, stronger relationships between industry players. The industry needs to forge a new links in the supply chains on the basis of deeper understandings of the respective businesses.

All parties in a supply chain must be willing to speak openly and listen attentively. They must also be willing to be much more transparent. That's the only way to cement greater trust.

Shell intends to align its internal processes to ensure the capital and labor efficiency of its projects. But for that to be successful, Shell's contractors need to align their processes, practices and performance incentives to the same end. He asked, "Will we come up with performance indicators we can all agree on? Do we have the courage to be transparent with those data? Can we admit where profits are being made? Where losses are being incurred?

Interestingly, even where we disagree, talking about it openly at least helps us to understand one another better. We can appreciate how we individually balance risks and rewards. And that's already a step forward".

Improving Capital Efficiency

These are trying times for the industry. And it is precisely at times like these that true leaders must stand up and act, setting shining examples for others to follow.

Each of companies is coping with its own troubles. Some of them are cyclical and will pass. But others have regrettably become ingrained in the industry's ways of working. They have become bad habits, and they will not go away when the oil price goes up or steel prices go down. ***They have to be eradicated once and for all through a wholesale transformation of the supply chain.*** And that comes down to industry leaders – linking their supply chains on the basis of a deeper understanding of the respective businesses and a deeper commitment to mutual success.

"Like those great industry leaders who brought the industry through perilous times in the late 80s, let's pull together to give the oil and gas industry the world-leading supply chain it needs", He calls.

USA Oil and Gas Monitor Subscription and Advert Rates

12 month Digital Subscription @ $119.88
12 month Print Subscription @ $144
Excludes taxes and shipping where applicable

New! *Our Digital Edition is distributed by Amazon Kindle Select- Guarantees 1 billion Audience Reach!*
Digital Edition Advert Rates
Full Page Advert $500
Half Page Advert $250

Print Edition Advert Rates
Full Page Advert $2000
Half Page Advert $1000
Quarter Page Advert $650

For Online Advert Placement
Go online @
www.usaoilandgasmonitor.com/advertise

Request more info by emailing us today or go to www.usaoilandgasmonitor.com/subscribe

Balancing CAPEX and OPEX along the Entire Value Chain- Siemens Solutions

Having Siemens experts involved early in the concept phase is the best possible start for a performance-driven solution. The result is the finest technical solutions offering high productivity, low lifecycle costs, and reduced project risks.

Considerable cost savings both on CAPEX and OPEX are achieved through customized package solutions that encompass entire functionalities.

Economical offshore drilling

Siemens stand for innovative solution packages for offshore drilling that secure reliable operation and availability. Siemens solutions are based on broad expertise in electrical, instrumentation, and telecommunication EIT, rotating equipment, and water treatment solutions, as well as years of hands-on experience in the oil and gas business and marine applications.

Siemens scope of supply covers the entire lifecycle of equipment and assets, thus ensuring long-term reliability and ideal investment protection. Moreover, thanks to long-standing business partnerships with leading shipyards, naval architects, and drilling service operators, we understand the needs and demands of the markets – and how to deliver exacting solutions

Utmost reliability for offshore production and processing

For all types of mobile units and jack-up rigs, we deliver proven solution packages for reliable operation and high availability – from power supply including fault-tolerant systems through drives for all applications to integrated process solutions for gas and water, as well as automation and management systems and marine systems.

Floating Production Units FPUs also call for the highest operational efficiency as well as an integrated design of all topside solutions. We can provide this, thanks to our cutting-edge technologies, our wealth of experience in furnishing FPUs, and our comprehensive lifecycle services, safeguarding the highest performance of all components at any time.

The key to subsea success: products, systems, and lifecycle services for Deepwater developments

Siemens enables enhanced recovery in the most challenging locations, covering everything from connectors and sensors to topside and onshore power supply, in-field subsea power distribution, control, surveillance, and processing technologies. Our portfolio includes subsea products, systems, and exemplary service and support.

Siemens subsea products include market-leading brands like Tronic, Matre, and Bennex. The reliable Tronic line of DigiTRON, SpecTRON, FoeTRON, and ElecTRON products provides electrical and fiber-optic connector systems for subsea power and communications.

Siemens Matre wellhead pressure sensors, pressure temperature sensors, and differential pressure transducers are renowned for delivering optimal performance and reliability. The Siemens subsea offering also includes high-performance Bennex equipment for power solutions, fiber optic, and seismic applications.

Reliable, optimized onshore production and processing

From wellhead to export, the Siemens Oil and Gas portfolio includes equipment for all stages of onshore production, including gas lift, gas treatment, export gas compression, and power supply. Dedicated compression solutions are available for dirty-gas applications, tight gas production, and for mature fields requiring a wide operating area. Completely integrated facility automation and control systems provide for consistent operations management from the local control room to the dispatching center. Moreover, the Siemens scope of supply covers the entire lifecycle of equipment and assets, ensuring long-term reliability and ideal investment protection.

Comprehensive solutions for unconventional gas

Tight gas, shale gas, and coal-bed methane will help meet the growing demand for natural gas in many regions of the world. With our unconventional gas portfolio, you can rely on tested and field-proven equipment for all production stages, including gas lift, gas treatment, gas gathering, export gas compression, power supply, water treatment, and the LNG process. Precisely adapted system components with proven performance right from start-up are the basis for all of our solutions. An integrated electrical solution from Siemens reduces the number of interfaces and therefore your production risks.

Safe and efficient gas and liquid pipelines

Pipelines are indispensable for the safe, reliable, and efficient transportation of oil and gas and represent a fundamental lifeline for every national economy. Siemens serves the customer as an independent consultant for partial FEED activities and as a provider of integrated solutions for gas pipeline machinery, automation, electrical, security, and communication systems. This enables Siemens to supply true one-stop solutions, which make a decisive contribution to the optimization of the total cost of ownership.

The clever solution: liquefied natural gas LNG

Partly due to growing global demand, LNG is becoming increasingly popular. To make LNG even more attractive, we have developed improvements to the reliability, efficiency, and environmental impact of the entire LNG process chain, allowing the cost-effective use of existing natural gas deposits anywhere in the world. Especially for LNG receiving terminals we offer a comprehensive energy supply, automation, drive, and IT approach – all from a single source. Dedicated plant packages include integrated automation and control solutions for unloading jetty, berthing, mooring, storage plant, storage tanks, boil-off gas compression, vaporizer systems, and send-out.

What's more, Siemens delivers boil-off gas BOG compression solutions of unparalleled performance. Documented by references, their innovative designs as well as their extraordinary durability and extended operating life made

Siemens the worldwide market leader in BOG recovery technology.

Tank farms and terminals

Tank farms play an important role in the logistics of crude oil and natural gas. Like underground gas storage, they can help reduce the impact of demand spikes, and are also an important energy trading tool. We can simplify your tank farm and terminal operations and reduce your operating costs. Integrating these assets into one of our supervisory control and data acquisition SCADA systems allows you to closely monitor all automated processes, providing quick problem identification and isolation, saving you time and money. Our portfolio includes automated loading systems, tank gauging, distribution planning, and batch management, blending, and rebranding facilities.

Reliable and economical: gas storage

Underground gas storage facilities are an essential part of all natural-gas planning and logistics. With a capacity of billions of cubic meters, they smooth out daily and seasonal swings in demand, and ensure that there will always be enough gas for customers at any time of year. Siemens solutions for underground gas storage include the full scope of rotating and electrical equipment needed to operate the facility. Compressors, gas turbines and e-drives are available with a wide range of power ratings to match specific volume flows and dynamics. Our globally recognized automation and control technology integrates all assets, ensuring maximum availability and efficiency of the complete station, and allowing fully remote-controlled operation.

Gas-to-liquid – a well-developed future technology

With rising crude oil prices and tightening environmental specifications for sulfur and aromatics in diesel fuel, gas-to-liquid GTL plants become ever more profitable. Their economics can be further improved by optimizing plant efficiency and availability.

Siemens is a prime supplier to many GTL projects around the world, providing high-power, high-volume compressor trains for such processes as the gas reforming stage or for the cryogenic separation process used to convert natural gas to syngas. What's more, with power generation and distribution, water management, automation and control, industrial IT, and lifecycle services all from a single source, we provide a host of solutions helping to integrate utilities, run plants at optimal levels of efficiency, and ensure maximum availability.

New levels of safety and efficiency for the refining and petrochemical industry

Keeping process safety up and operating costs down, and ensuring a reliable and continuous power supply: Those are the major challenges in the refining industry today. We answer them with our comprehensive technology portfolio, featuring field-proven compressors and drive solutions for just about any refinery process, from fluid catalytic cracking, hydrocracking, and coking to platforming, sulfur recovery, and hydro treating.

This is complemented by our range of fire and gas systems, emergency shutdown safety systems, and our pressure relief systems management service, while our economical and dependable power supply solutions guarantee power throughout your plant, right down to the motors and consumer terminals.

As a market leader in rotating equipment for methanol, olefin, and ammonia production, we can offer compressor trains for virtually all your needs, including crack gas, refrigeration, feed gas, synthesis gas, charge gas, recycle gas, natural gas, and CO_2. To help you operate your processes and plants with maximum efficiency, our distributed control systems DCS integrate all associated process instrumentation and integrated data visualization software.

Harish Patel- Director of Technology, Drilling and Production

ABS put BAVO Requirements into Perspective as Well Control Safety Rule enters Implementation Stage

USAOGM: *Harish Patel- tell us about yourself- what you do at ABS?*

ABS: I am the Director of Technology, Drilling and Production. I have more than 25 years of industry experience related to design analysis of wellheads, well control, drilling equipment, pressure vessels, hydrocarbon production and processing equipment. I also have extensive experience in risk identification and have carried out special studies on innovative and novel offshore concepts. Today at ABS, I am responsible for developing requirements for classification of drilling systems, systematic validation of new technology for various field applications and risk evaluations. As Technology Director, I help to develop and publish requirements for classification/certification of technology used in applications including dual gradient drilling and managed pressure drilling, CNG carriers, and floating LNG facilities. I have a Master of Engineering degree in Mechanical Engineering from Stevens Institute of Technology.

USAOGM: *Regarding the new well control safety rule- what is ABS position/role regarding this rule and how can your service offering help the industry comply easily with this rule.*

ABS: New Safety rules require verification by a BSEE Approved Verification Organization BAVO prior to use of certain equipment such as BOPs and other well control equipment.

The final regulation improves the previous requirements for inspection, maintenance, and repair of this equipment. The final regulation requires an annual Mechanical Integrity Assessment Report to be completed on certain BOPs by a BSEE approved verification organization. This report includes, but is not limited to, BOP repair and maintenance records, documentation of the equipment service life, and a comprehensive assessment of the overall system. This creates complete traceability for equipment even if it is serviced or repaired in a foreign jurisdiction.

The final regulation contains a performance requirement that the equipment be maintained pursuant to Original Equipment Manufacturer OEM requirements, good engineering practices, and industry standards. It also includes personnel training requirements for repairs and maintenance.

The final regulation also includes, as a regulatory requirement, the complete breakdown and detailed physical inspection of the BOP at intervals not longer than every 5 years. The complete breakdown and inspection can be performed in phased intervals.

As an independent organization, ABS has experienced people available to deliver all of the services required under the new safety rule. The intent of the proposed additional requirement is to improve safety, protect life and the natural environment, which is ABS' mission also. ABS believes that BAVO, and the expertise and experience that come with it, will improve offshore safety.

USAOGM: *Is ABS a BAVO for this well control safety regulation? If yes, how simple and burdensome will this yearly paper work cost operators. Will it require them hiring new staff- put in place a new kind of software?*

ABS: Current regulations require I3P verification. BSEE changed the terminology to BAVO and additional requirements have been added to the regulations. Cost impact won't be dramatic for I3P verification, but it is expected to increase due to additional requirements. Operators still need to maintain and document veering irrespective job BAVO requirements. All of the documents need to be independently verified by a third party. If an operator is doing everything correctly and maintaining all records, documentation will have a minimum cost impact. By requiring I3P verification for current regulations, this will improve safety efforts in the industry.

USAOGM: *What is ABS Offering the oil and gas industry that can help the industry adapt in this low oil price environment?*

ABS: The primary focus for ABS is safety. We develop guidance for industry that keeps pace with technology advancement, which we do by talking often with clients. Our goal is for our guidance to be appropriate, relevant and practical. Our newest guide is an example. It addresses laying up rigs so they can quickly re-enter service. It is this kind of guidance that helps the oil and gas industry cope with difficult situations with confidence. Companies look to ABS as a trusted advisor.

USAOGM: *What new technology services – ABS is bringing into the industry at this time?*

ABS: We are working closely with companies developing managed pressure drilling technology, with manufacturers of equipment for HP/HT operations. And we are focusing on what we refer to as FutureClass™, an approach to inspection that is risk-based, continuous, and less intrusive. To accomplish that, we are investing in CyberSecurity, which extends to integrated software quality management, data management and data analytics, and new inspection technologies like drones and a hardhat that is equipped with a camera. We invest in technology because that is what gives us an edge in developing industry guidance and helping to solve challenges. ABS is a technology leader.

BSEE held a press conference at OTC 2016 to provide updates on agency activities, recognize the winners of the first annual High School Technology Challenge, and announce a hiring push

BSEE Timeline for Implementation of the Well Control Rule

BSEE understands that operators may need time to comply with certain requirements in this rule. Based on input from many in the oil and gas industry, all new drilling rigs are being built pursuant to the same industry standards BSEE has adopted, and many have already been retrofitted to comply with these industry standards. Furthermore, most comply with recognized engineering practices and OEM requirements related to repair and training. BSEE has established an effective date of 3 months following publication of the final rule. Operators are required to demonstrate compliance with most of the requirements at that time, with the exception of the following more extended timeframes:

- Operators are required to install a gas bleed line with two valves for the annular preventer no later than 2 years from publication of the final rule
- Operators are required have the capability to shear and seal tubing with exterior control lines no later than 2 years from the publication of the final rule.

- The BOP is required to be able to shear electric-, wire-, and slick-line no later than 2 years after publication of the final rule.
- Operators are required to use BSEE Approved Verification Organizations BAVOs no later than 1 year from the date when BSEE publishes the list of BAVOs.
- Operators are required to comply with the real-time monitoring requirements within 3 years from the publication of the final rule.
- Operators are required to install remotely-controlled locks on surface BOP sealing rams no later than 3 years from publication of the final rule.
- Operators are required to have dedicated subsea accumulator capacity for auto shear and Deadman functions on subsea BOPs within 5 years from the publication of the final rule.
- Operators are required to install dual shear rams on subsea BOPs within 5 years from the publication of the final rule.
- Surface BOPs installed on floating facilities 3 years after publication of the final rule must comply with the dual shear ram requirement.
- Operators are required to install a mechanism coupled with each shear rams that centers drill pipe during shearing operations within 7 years from the publication of the final rule.
- For any risers installed 90 days after the date of the publication of the final rule or later, operators are required to use dual bore risers for surface BOPs on floating production facilities.

Finally, the major differences in the final rule:

Significant Differences between the Proposed and Final Rules:

1. Safe drilling margin - The static downhole mud weight must be a minimum of 0.5 pound per gallon PPG below the lesser of the casing shoe pressure integrity test or the lowest estimated fracture gradient "the 0.5 PPG drilling margin". However, the use of an alternative to the 0.5 PPG drilling margin is acceptable if the operator submits and receives approval based on adequate justification and documentation, including supplemental data, in their Application for Permit to Drill.
2. Accumulator systems - We require that subsea accumulators have enough capacity to provide pressure for critical functions, as defined in API Standard 53, and to have accumulator bottles that are dedicated to auto shear and Deadman functions but not EDS, and that may be shared between those functions.
3. BOP 5-year major inspection - Based on consideration of the issues raised in the comments, BSEE has revised the final rule in order to allow a phased approach for five-year inspections e.g., staggered inspection for each component, as long as there is proper documentation and tracking to ensure that BSEE can verify that each applicable BOP component has had the major inspection within five years.
4. Real-time monitoring RTM plan requirement - The RTM requirements will be based upon a particular rig configuration and situation, and RTM is intended to be used as a support tool for the existing rig-based chain of command and is not a substitute for the competency or well-control responsibilities of the rig personnel. The final rule now requires operators to have a RTM plan that includes procedures for responding to and notifying BSEE of "significant and/or prolonged interruptions." The Bureau will still have access to RTM data and facilities upon request.
5. Potential Increased Severing Capability - This provision has been removed entirely from the rule. There were very few comments received on that provision during the public comment period, and the Bureau feels that more time may be needed to assess both the current state of severing capabilities, as well as alternative technologies that may currently be under development. The Bureau is committed to reviewing this under EO 13563.
6. BOP Pressure Testing Interval –The proposed 14-day pressure testing requirement for BOPs used in all types of operations has been finalized in the rule. Additional studies, data collection and analysis, and risk assessments will be needed to produce a reasonable foundation for BSEE to determine whether to revise either to increase or decrease the uniform 14-day testing interval. In the meantime, any operator that believes its specific circumstances warrant a longer pressure test interval may seek approval from the District Manager to use alternate procedures or equipment under existing regulations.

Thunder Series continues Gardner Denver's legacy of leading with innovative technology

Gardner Denver Unveils Next-Generation Frac Pump at OTC

Gardner Denver, a leading provider of petroleum and industrial pumps for more than 150 years, debuted its latest innovation with the Thunder Series frac pump at the Offshore Technology Conference OTC. Gardner Denver invented the original frac pump more than 60 years ago and continues that legacy of innovation with this latest announcement. The debut of this pump represents Gardner Denver's commitment to continuous improvement, revolutionary technologies and listening to the voice of the customer.

The Thunder series frac pump is designed to meet the challenges of today's frac operations. With increasing pressures and 24/7 pumping duty cycles, customers are demanding equipment that can operate on longer maintenance intervals. Based on the GD-3000 pump platform, which is field proven in the most severe shale plays, the Thunder series pump uses long stroke technology to operate at lower speeds while enhancing flow rate capabilities. This extends the pump's maintenance overhaul life cycle, while also reducing consumables and associated labor costs by $250,000 over the life of the pump.

"The Thunder series is our response to listening to our customers around the industry," said Larry Kerr, VPGM, Gardner Denver Petroleum and Industrial Pumps. "They asked for a pump that operates more efficiently, with longer product life, and ultimately saves them money. The Thunder series was designed for performance and serviceability and demonstrates our commitment to innovation and meeting customer needs regardless of the current price environment."

This next-generation frac pump utilizes innovative technology to improve performance and reduce the total cost of ownership:

- The Thunder Series significantly improves wear and tear resistance, allowing the power end maintenance overhaul to be consistent with engine, pump and transmission maintenance service schedules.
- The enhanced power end technology makes maintenance easier and safer, thus reducing downtime.
- Thunder next-generation technology increases fluid end life by three times.
- Designed for optimum performance, the Thunder Series includes a triplex pump that reaches 2,550 brake horsepower BHP while the quintuplex pump reaches 3,000 BHP.

Gardner Denver also provides customers with the full circle of service and support, or Gardner Denver's Experience 360, to help customers maximize uptime through product training, parts on demand, customer service and repair, from the point of sale to the end of the pump's life.

Seven New DNV GL Collaborative Projects in North America

OTC Houston: In a concerted drive to find smart solutions to safely reduce complexities and cost in the North American oil and gas industry, DNV GL is leading seven new joint industry projects JIP from the region in 2016. The initiatives will support overall efficiency efforts in the pipelines, wells and subsea, umbilicals, risers, and flowlines SURF sectors.

Key focus areas for DNV GL in 2016 will be centered on solving challenges around standardization, operations OPEX services, safety, environment, regulations and performance.

"Our collaborative projects are pivotal in strengthening the industry throughout the Americas and helping it move forward and out of the difficulties we are currently facing," said Peter Bjerager, Executive vice president, Oil & Gas – DNV GL Region Americas. "As an independent third party we are uniquely positioned to provide a neutral ground for collaboration."

DNV GL is inviting industry players to take part in the following JIPs:

- Extended application of corrosion resistant alloys
- Guidance for qualifying materials in compliance with API 17TR8 HPHT design guidelines for subsea equipment
- Increased consistency for sour service testing and assessment
- Sour HPHT fatigue testing for clad subsea components
- Prediction of internal flow induced vibration of complex subsea pipework
- Jumper VIV instrumentation and field measurements - expanding ongoing JIP
- Safe assessment of embedded flaws in sour pipelines

According to a recent research report published by DNV GL1, one-third of North American respondents are concerned that they do not have a strategy in place to maintain innovation in a declined market. However, 31% see greater involvement in JIPs as a priority over the next 12 months, while four in ten want to increase collaboration with other industry players 40 per cent.

The report also found that six out of ten 60 per cent respondents agreed that operators will increasingly push to standardize their approach globally- up from 42 per cent in 2015. Only 9 per cent expect an increase in spending in R&D and innovation, a figure that has been cut by more than half in two years, from 20 per cent in 2014.

"Like the global oil and gas industry, companies in North America are braced for an extended period of lower oil prices, which is leading to continued pressure on cost management. However, it is encouraging that there is still enthusiasm to work together and drive greater standardization and reduce inefficiencies. The success of our collaborative approach has seen the introduction

USA Oil and Gas Monitor
For Daily News Report and Analysis • www.usaoilandgasmonitor.com

of new industry standards and practices which help advance innovation and reduce complexity," continued Peter Bjerager.

In total, 43 DNV GL-led JIPs have been initiated globally this year, in addition to the launch of a new Step Change innovation program to help customers leverage opportunities from digitalization.

DNV GL's 'Technology Outlook 2025' report predicts and showcases technology trends across a number of industries. For oil and gas, key developments include digitalization, connectivity, automation and remote operation.

A New Reality: the outlook for the oil and gas industry in 2016 is an industry benchmark study from DNV GL, the leading technical advisor to the industry. Now in its sixth year, the program builds on the findings of five prior annual outlook reports, first launched in early 2011. During October and November 2015, we surveyed 921 senior professionals and executives across the global oil and gas industry. More than a third 35 per cent of respondents work for oil and gas operators, while 60 per cent are employed by suppliers and service companies across the industry. The remaining respondents come from regulators and trade associations. The companies surveyed vary in size: 40 per cent had annual revenue of USD 500m or less, while 14 per cent had annual revenue in excess of USD 10bn. Respondents were drawn from publicly-listed companies and privately-held firms. They also represent a range of functions within the industry, from board-level executives to senior engineers.

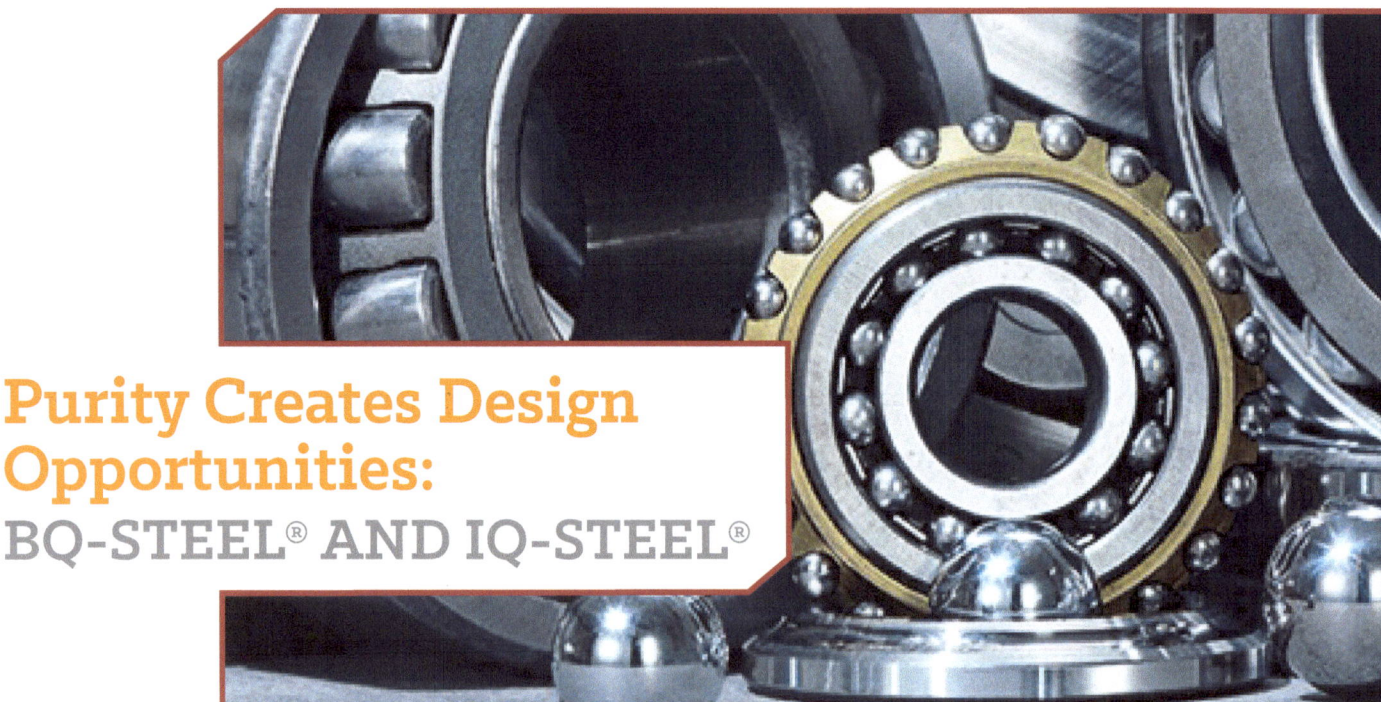

Purity Creates Design Opportunities:
BQ-STEEL® AND IQ-STEEL®

IQ-Steel® Isotropic Quality is an isotropic quality ultra clean steel whereas BQ-Steel® Bearing Quality is a bearing quality clean steel. They are both optimized for fatigue strength by a strict control of steel cleanliness. IQ-Steel is a smart solution for designing reliable components that can take the strain from higher and more complex loads. It offers uniform and excellent properties in all loading directions. BQ-Steel is also ideal for new design solutions in a wide array of demanding applications outside the bearing industry that require longer performance and higher loads.

Key Benefits
- Consistent high quality
- Superior service life
- Macroscopic cleanliness control with immersion ultrasonic testing
- Based on 100 years knowledge of bearing steel manufacturing

In simple load cases the bending fatigue strength can typically be increased by 30 to 90 percent, depending on the steel used today. In multi-axial load cases increases of up to 70 percent can be achieved.

Control from start to finish

By controlling the entire chain of production, from melt to rolling and final component, we can guarantee precise results.

To verify the result we use front-end test and inspection methods to secure the demands of high cleanliness and enable lighter and stronger solutions.

As part of the process, we verify that the quality of the BQ-Steel® will result in superior fatigue properties. Rotating bending fatigue testing is an important and frequently used technique.

BQ-Steel and IQ-Steel have significantly smaller inclusions sizes compared to conventional steel. Note how the curve in the upper-left-hand corner is much steeper, meaning that the gain in fatigue strength is increasing exponentially.

Customized for each customer's needs

Designs in engineering steel are in most cases subject to cyclic stress during a long period of time. This makes fatigue normally the limiting property. From experience it is known that defects such as non-metallic inclusions will initiate fatigue failures. The required stress is significantly lower than the yield or fracture strength, in other words, the static strength.

The effect of reduced inclusion sizes in BQ-Steel makes it typically utilized to get weight reduction on existing generations of end-user systems. Moderate design changes can also be made while securing high and consistent quality level for the end-user products. The effect on fatigue by applying BQ-Steel is visualized in the graph below.

The smart choice

BQ-Steel is normally the first comparison when upgrading from conventional steel. As the properties of BQ-Steel are applicable to almost all steel grades there is no end-user application that can be excluded.

BQ-Steel® – exceeding present fatigue limits

With a steelmaking legacy stretching back 400 years, we've also been providing premium bearing-quality steel to leading OEMS for 100 years. Initially developed to overcome fatigue strength issues in bearing assemblies, our BQ-Steel is now available for all types of applications involving fatigue loads.

By reducing the size of inclusions in BQ-Steel, it is now possible to use less material to achieve the same strength and thus lower the total weight. As a result, moderate design changes can also be made while securing a high and consistent quality level for the end-user products. BQ-Steel grades open up design possibilities by increasing fatigue strength by 30–90 % compared with conventional steel.

IQ-Steel® – toward maximum fatigue strength

IQ-Steel is our smart solution to the need for designing reliable components that can take the strain from higher and more complex loads. The superior isotropic properties of the steel are opening new design possibilities. For example, in simple load cases the bending fatigue strength can typically be increased by 40–100 per cent, in the case of a multi-axial load designs, fatigue limitations can be reduced by 130 per cent, enabling significant size or weight reductions.

When benchmarking our IQ-Steel against more expensive vacuum arc re-melting VAR steel, we could see that they were equal or superior in terms of materials properties and performance. Today, BQ-Steel and IQ-Steel are available for many more grades than just bearing steels.

USA Oil and Gas Monitor
For Daily News Report and Analysis • www.usaoilandgasmonitor.com

Bearing Up In Oil and Gas
Help Cut Downtime and Boost Reliability

SKF's new design of tapered roller thrust bearings will boost the reliability of top drives, says Roland Muttenthaler, Business Development Manager at SKF Gothenburg, Sweden, 5 May, 2016: In the oil and gas industry, reliability is key to success. Unexpected downtime due to machinery or component failure results in massive cost both onshore and offshore sectors.

US regulations require that equipment used in the oil and gas industry is maintained every five years. Operators in the industry wish that their equipment would last this long: because of the punishing conditions and extreme environment, servicing is required long before the five-year period is up. Most often, after a few years only an overhaul is needed.

SKF has optimized a number of its products to make them appropriate for use in the oil and gas industry. One recent example is an improved tapered roller thrust bearing for top drives, which can help to prolong service intervals and save money.

The top drive – a critical mechanism that forms part of a drilling rig, generates enormous forces. As a consequence, the main internal thrust bearings must withstand extreme conditions: high shock loads, axial loads and possible shaft and housing deflections. At the same time, the combination of heavy loads and low speeds at extreme temperatures pushes the lubrication conditions to the limit –leading to faster wear.

SKF's redesigned tapered roller thrust bearings can better overcome the above problems, helping to improve the performance and reliability of top drives. This is all the more important, considering that drill rigs are drilling deeper than ever before, putting higher demands on the equipment. One of the main causes of failure is excessive shock loads on the gearbox – and that is what the new bearing is designed to resist.

> SKF's redesigned tapered roller thrust bearings can better overcome the above problems, helping to improve the performance and reliability of top drives.

Outward appearance

There is no outward difference in the bearing's appearance. In fact, it will look very similar to many competitive products. However, the devil is in the detail: advanced simulation helped SKF to fine-tune the internal geometry, giving the bearing the highest possible load rating.

One element is a new cage design. Using a pin-type cage – rather than a standard brass cage – allows more rollers to fit within the bearing, and thus withstand a greater load. That said, many customers will be fine with a brass cage – as the pin-type cage will be for extreme applications.

Other key design changes include optimizing the logarithmic profile, which balances load distribution along each roller. At the same time, rollers are designed to be virtually identical to one another – reducing stress peaks on single rollers, as well as cutting noise and vibration.

While design changes were the key factor behind the performance of the new bearing, some manufacturing changes were also crucial. Enhancing the surface finish by using a different type of coating can help the bearing withstand the effect of marginal lubrication in extreme operating conditions. Drilling often takes place at -40 degrees C -40F, which can cause the lubricant to thicken. This, combined with high loads, can affect correct lubrication – leading to bearing damage. The advanced surface finish maximizes the effect of the lubricant, reducing excessive friction and damage to the bearing contacts.

It's important to note that the improved performance is achieved using standard quality SKF steel. For similar performance improvements, competitors are forced to use enhanced material specifications.

SKF has spent significant amount of time developing the new bearing design. It began by analyzing SKF bearings that had been used in the field, in an attempt to understand – and overcome – any wear patterns that it found on them. Later, improved designs were modelled using simulation software. The optimized and improved design was validated by simulation tools and field tests.

In addition to these new tapered roller thrust bearings, SKF will showcase two other important bearing innovations at OTC 2016: Kaydon slewing ring bearings; and a sensor bearing unit. Both are appropriate for use in top drives.

Its Kaydon slewing ring bearings can be used in the pipe handling system that is fixed to the bottom of the gearbox of the top drive. Many OEMs save money by making a 'tailor made' version using a standard bearing and adding some tooth gears. A better solution is to use a slewing ring bearing with integrated gear, which can help cut failures in the pipe handler.

At the same time, its sensor bearing unit can be used in the top drive's motor. The product was originally used in the railway industry, but has been adapted for oil and gas – including a version for top drives. The single unit replaces a bearing and an encoder – and is thus more compact and robust.

Top drives are a critical part of any oil and gas operation, and anything that can improve them – such as these bearing innovations – will help to cut downtime and boost reliability.

> SKF has optimized a number of its products to make them appropriate for use in the oil and gas industry. One recent example is an improved tapered roller thrust bearing for top drives, which can help to prolong service intervals and save money.

USA Oil and Gas Monitor
For Daily News Report and Analysis • www.usaoilandgasmonitor.com

USA Oil and Gas Monitor
For Daily News Report and Analysis • www.usaoilandgasmonitor.com

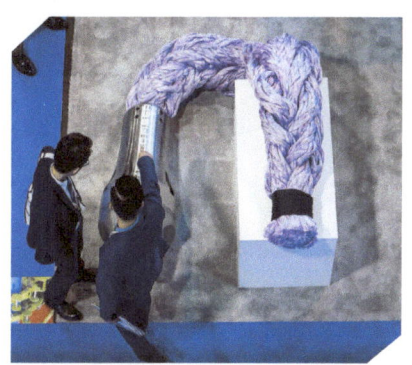

www.ingramcontent.com/pod-product-compliance
Lightning Source LLC
Chambersburg PA
CBHW050420180526
45159CB00005B/2348